I0814946

CITY CRITTERS
Pigeons
by Betsy Rathburn
BLASTOFF! READERS
1
BELLWETHER MEDIA • MINNEAPOLIS, MN

Blastoff! Readers are carefully developed by literacy experts to build reading stamina and move students toward fluency by combining standards-based content with developmentally appropriate text.

Level 1 provides the most support through repetition of high-frequency words, light text, predictable sentence patterns, and strong visual support.

Level 2 offers early readers a bit more challenge through varied sentences, increased text load, and text-supportive special features.

Level 3 advances early-fluent readers toward fluency through increased text load, less reliance on photos, advancing concepts, longer sentences, and more complex special features.

★ **Blastoff! Universe**

Reading Level

Grade K

Grades 1–3

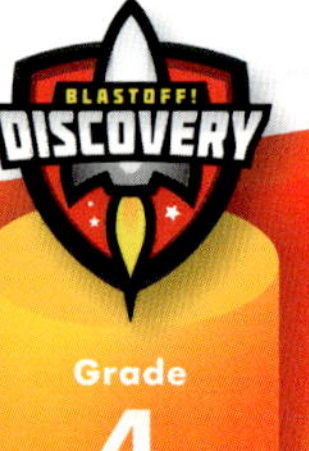

Grade 4

This edition first published in 2025 by Bellwether Media, Inc.

Library of Congress Cataloging-in-Publication Data

Names: Rathburn, Betsy, author.
Title: Pigeons / by Betsy Rathburn.
Description: Minneapolis, MN : Bellwether Media, 2025. | Series: Blastoff! Readers: City Critters | Includes bibliographical references and index. | Audience: Ages 5-8 | Audience: Grades K-1 | Summary: "Developed by literacy experts for students in kindergarten through grade three, this book introduces pigeons in cities to young readers through leveled text and related photos"– Provided by publisher.
Identifiers: LCCN 2024035380 (print) | LCCN 2024035381 (ebook) | ISBN 9798893042184 (library binding) | ISBN 9798893043150 (ebook)
Subjects: LCSH: Pigeons–Juvenile literature. | Urban animals–Juvenile literature.
Classification: LCC QL696.C63 R38 2025 (print) | LCC QL696.C63 (ebook) | DDC 636.5/96–dc23/eng/20240809
LC record available at https://lccn.loc.gov/2024035380
LC ebook record available at https://lccn.loc.gov/2024035381

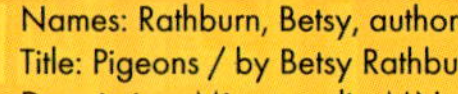

Editor: Christina Leaf   Designer: Gabriel Hilger

Printed in the United States of America, North Mankato, MN.

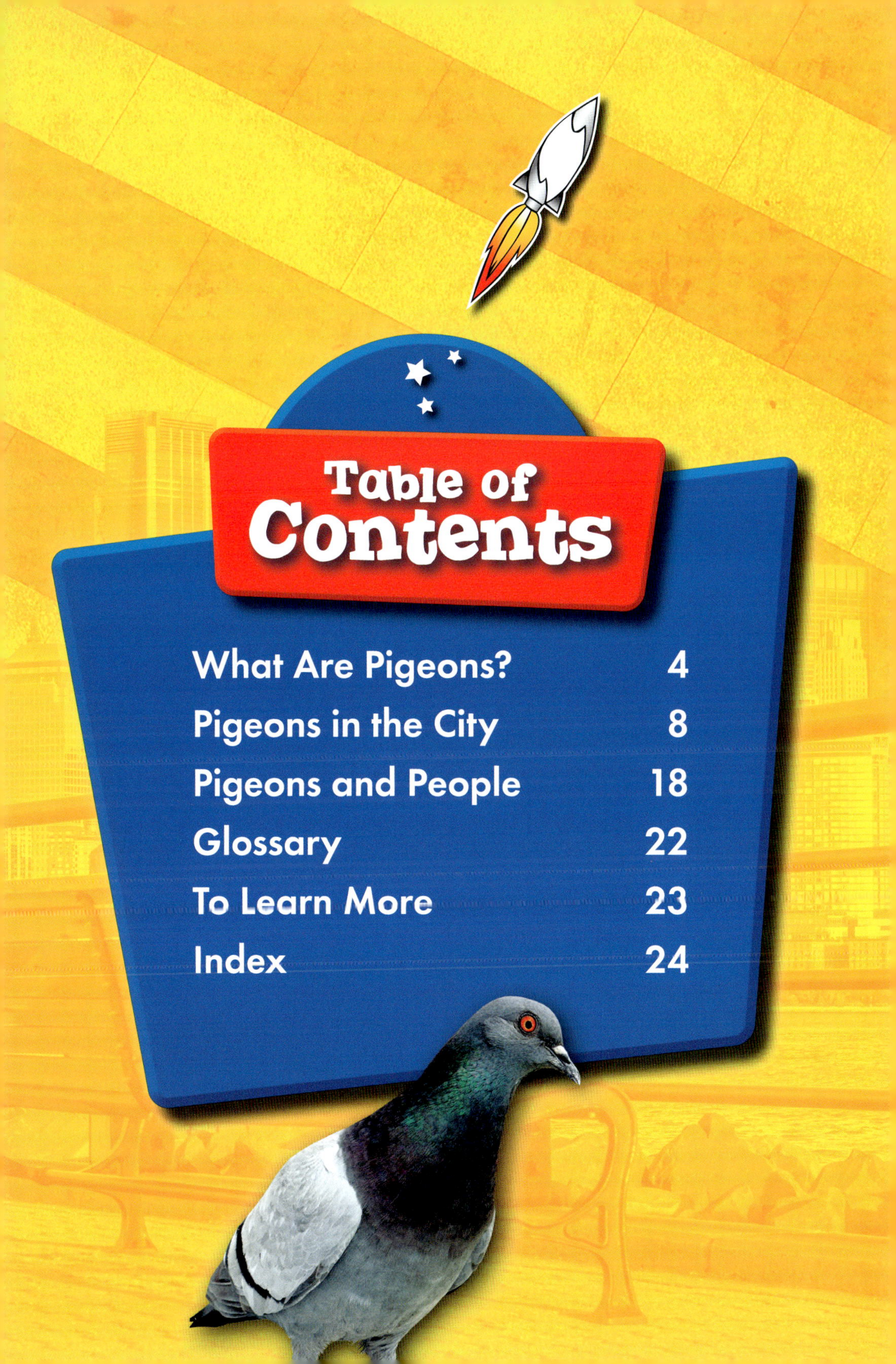

Table of Contents

What Are Pigeons?

Pigeons are birds.
There are many kinds.
Rock pigeons live
in cities!

Common City Pigeon
rock pigeon

Rock pigeons are gray. Most have shiny **feathers**. They have red feet and black **beaks**.

beak
shiny feathers

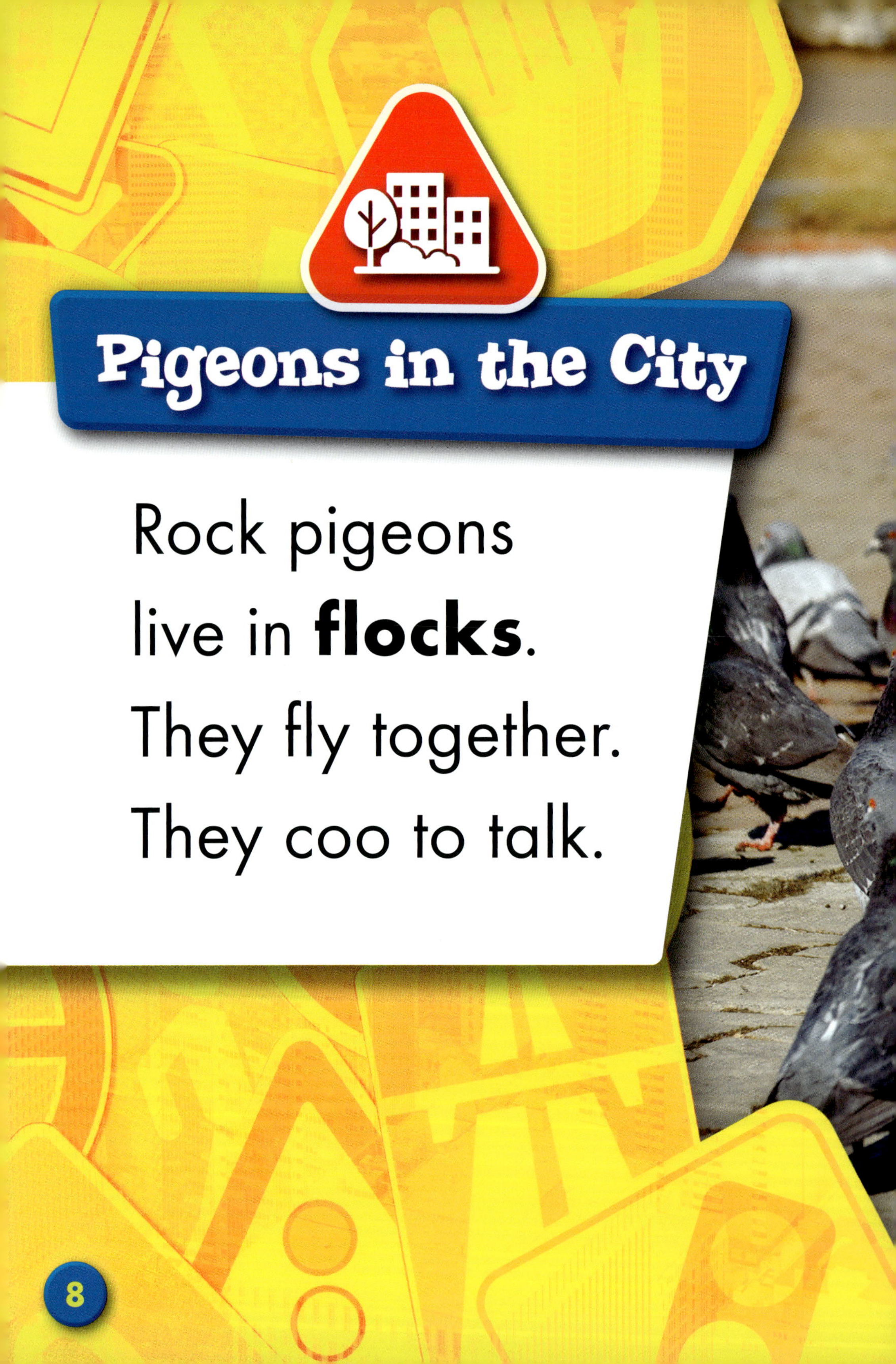

Pigeons in the City

Rock pigeons
live in **flocks**.
They fly together.
They coo to talk.

flock

They **perch** up high. They sit on stoplights and power lines.

perching

They look for seeds and bugs to eat. They eat people food, too.

Pigeon Food
seeds
bugs
people food

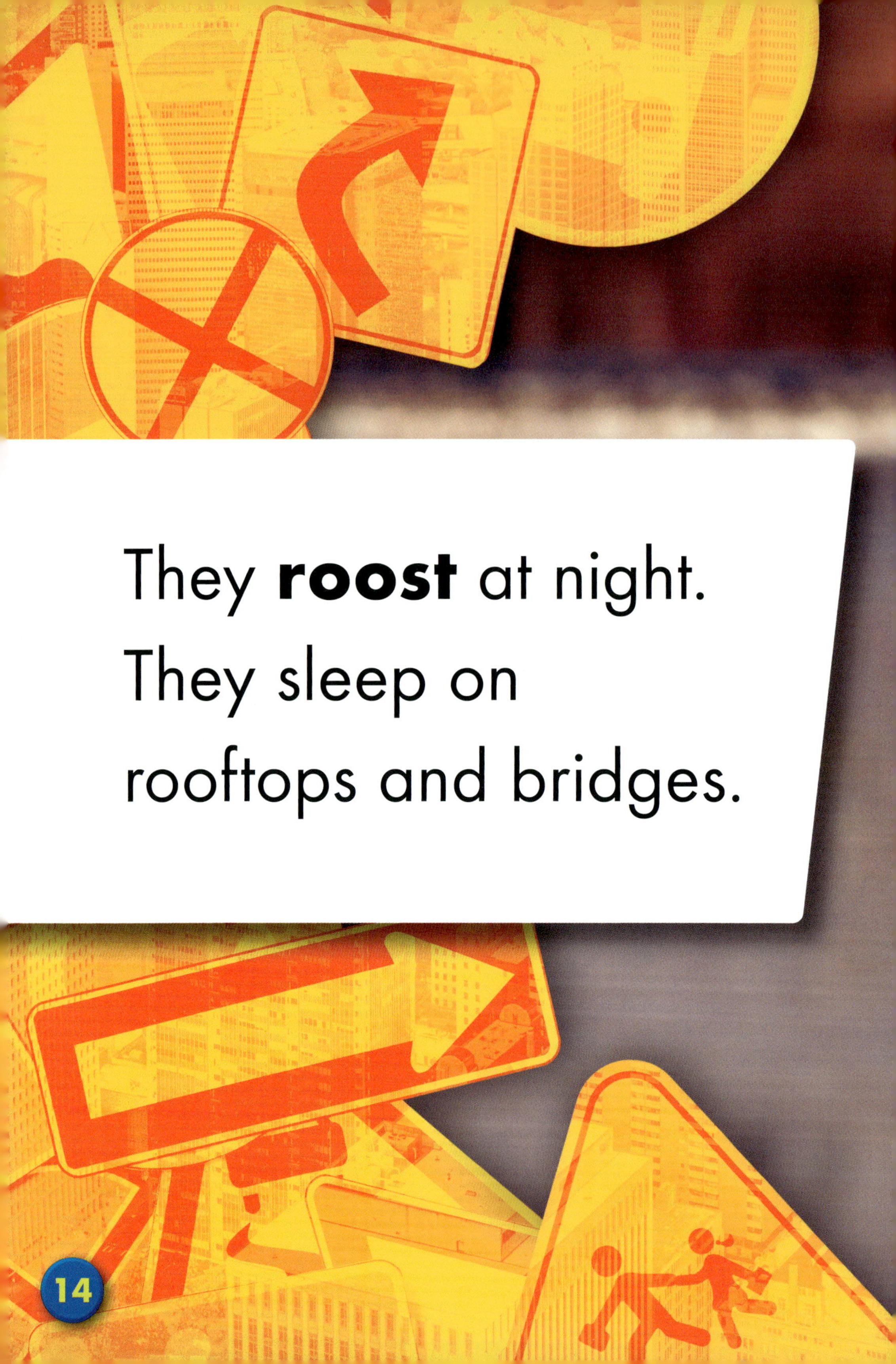

They **roost** at night.
They sleep on
rooftops and bridges.

roosting
Pigeon Homes
rooftops
bridges

Pairs make nests. Females lay eggs in them. Babies **hatch** and grow up.

hatching
nest

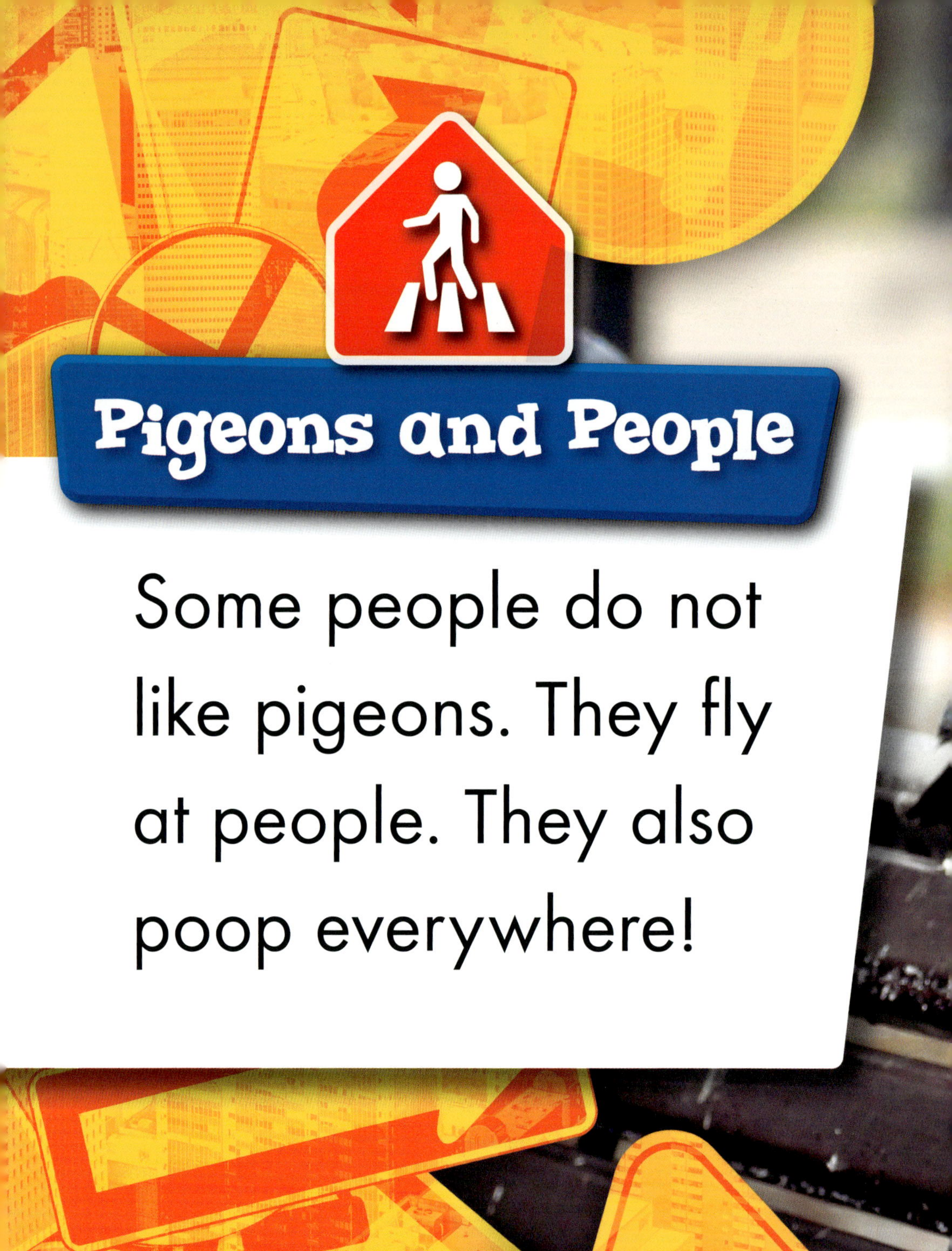

Pigeons and People

Some people do not like pigeons. They fly at people. They also poop everywhere!

poop

Other people like to feed them. These birds live well in cities!

Glossary

beaks

the hard front parts of the mouths of birds

hatch

to break out of an egg

feathers

light, soft coverings on birds' bodies

perch

to sit in a high place

flocks

groups of birds that live, travel, or feed together

roost

to rest in a high place

To Learn More

AT THE LIBRARY

Carney, Elizabeth. *Animals in the City.* Washington, D.C.: National Geographic Kids, 2019.

Mayntz, Melissa. *Birds for Kids: A Junior Scientist's Guide to Owls, Eagles, Penguins, and Other Bird Species.* Naperville, Ill.: Callisto Publishing, 2024.

Podmorow, Ava. *Pigeons: Animals in the City.* Oliver, B.C.: Engage Books, 2022.

ON THE WEB

FACTSURFER

Factsurfer.com gives you a safe, fun way to find more information.

1. Go to www.factsurfer.com.
2. Enter "pigeons" into the search box and click 🔍.
3. Select your book cover to see a list of related content.

Index

The images in this book are reproduced through the courtesy of: nermem, front cover (pigeon); Nikolay Lub, front cover (city); Gallinago_media, p. 3; Mike Workman, pp. 4-5; Ganga Raj Sunuwar, p. 5 (rock pigeon); Viktor Bunin, pp. 6-7; Sunil Iodhwal, p. 7 (shiny feathers); Sergey Borisov_88, pp. 8-9; MBurnham, pp. 10-11; Ashok Mehta, pp. 12-13; Martin Lisner, p. 13 (seeds); ag1100, p. 13 (bugs); Vladyslav Horoshevych, p. 13 (people food); Roman Bjuty, pp. 14-15; Wirestock Creators, p. 15 (rooftops); kamira777, p. 15 (bridges); Antonina Maistruk, pp. 16-17; gpetric, p. 17 (nest); Pixie Image, pp. 18-19; JabaWeba, pp. 20-21; Colin Seddon, p. 22 (beaks); Thanan Kongdoung, p. 22 (feathers); Purushottam Malav, p. 22 (flocks); Koonsiri Boonnak, p. 22 (hatch); Chris Mercer, p. 22 (perch); Phil Semmens, p. 22 (roost).